THE INVISIBLE $100 MILLION

by

BRIAN B. TURNER

This book is a work of nonfiction. While it references historical events, policies, and systemic patterns, any personal anecdotes or illustrative narratives are used for explanatory purposes. The views expressed are those of the author and are intended for informational and educational discussion. The book does not constitute legal, financial, or investment advice.

For permissions requests, inquiries, or more information, contact:

Published by HEY BBT LLC
www.heybbt.com

ISBN (Paperback): *978-1-971050-12-6*
ISBN (Hardcover): *978-1-971050-13-3*
ISBN (eBook): *978-1-971050-11-9*

First Edition

Printed in the United States

Table of Contents

INTRODUCTION

The Money That Was Never There

He stands in a quiet gym on a Tuesday night, long after the kids have gone home.
The lights hum. The floor is dusty. The scoreboard stays dark.

He wipes down the bench without thinking. It is a habit from years of muscle memory. He locks up the same way he once closed out arenas in front of forty thousand fans. Back then, every dunk, every steal, every step was broadcast to the world.

Tonight, no one is watching.
And that is the part the world never shows.

A few years ago, he was the name on everyone's timeline.
A draft pick with a smile built for TV.
A campus legend whose jersey once filled the student section in waves of matching color.

The stadium once roared his name.
The world slowly forgot his face.

He walks out to the parking lot, and for a moment, his breath catches.
The Bentley he used to drive is gone.
Tonight, he unlocks a Kia that serves the same purpose. Both get you where you need to go. Only one reminds you that the cheering was temporary.

He is not a tragedy.
He is the truth.
He is one story among thousands, each with a different path and the same ending.

This is where the curve ends for most of them. Not on a yacht. Not in the tabloids. Not in a mansion. The curve ends in a quiet restart where no camera crew shows up. The same machine that sold his rise has no use for the calm and unmarketable slope of his return to normal life.

This is the part that bothers people when they finally see it.
Not the fall, but the silence that comes after the spotlight fades.

The media loves two stories equally.
The miracle and the collapse.
Both sell. Both get clicks. Both feed the cycle.

They celebrate a teenager as a prodigy. Later, they mock him as a cautionary tale.
They replay his highlights in slow motion. Late,r they replay his bankruptcy filings with the same dramatic music.
They profit from the rise and profit again from the collapse.

Everyone loved the story when it helped them escape their own lives.
No one stayed when he needed help rebuilding his.

What the media never explains, and what they never pause to consider, is why the collapse is so common.
Why a system filled with billion-dollar stadiums, million-dollar coaches, and multimillion-dollar TV contracts produces a generation of athletes who walk away with less stability than the institutions they made rich.

The easy explanation is always the same.
He blew it.
He wasted his money.
He should have been smarter.

The truth is quieter and much heavier.

Most of these men never had the money people think they had.
They touched it, yes.
But they never held it.

Long before they signed a contract, the system had already claimed its share.
Through the grooming pipeline.
Through the NIL frenzy.
Through the draft day machine.
Through the cultural rescue role.
Through the hidden Black Tax.
Through predatory advisors.
Through invisible debts and expectations.
Through the belief that their success belonged to everyone around them.

He was built for the spotlight and praised for what his body could do. He was applauded for what he represented.
He was never taught the game that actually mattered.
The game behind the game.
The ownership game.
The only game that lasts longer than the cheers.

When the checks stopped, the machine did not slow down.
It simply moved on to the next young prospect, the next miracle, the next storyline that could be sold.

He was left here, in a quiet gym on a Tuesday night, restarting a life everyone assumed he had already won.

To understand how this happens, and to understand why even one hundred million dollars can vanish in plain sight, and to understand why the applause is temporary while the financial fallout is generational, we have to go back to the beginning.

We have to look before the contract.
Before the draft.
Before the spotlight.

The story does not start with the millions.
It starts in childhood.
It starts in the grooming.
It starts in the pipeline.

It starts long before the world is watching, on the part of the curve no one ever talks about.

The story begins on the part of the curve no one ever sees, because the money everyone talks about was never really there to begin with.

CHAPTER 1: THE GROOMING PIPELINE

Ten

He was ten years old the first time a grown man pointed at him the way scouts point at prospects. The gym was too loud for him to hear the full conversation, but he saw the gesture.
The nod.
The quiet smile.
The whisper that traveled down the sideline.

He thought they were impressed that he made a layup off the wrong foot.
In their minds, they were already imagining him at sixteen.

At ten, a child sees a basketball or a football as a toy.
Adults around him see possibility.
The system sees inventory.

He did not know that the moment his name was written on a clipboard, he had entered something much bigger than a game.

The Glitz Begins

Before he understood what was happening, people began to show up for him.

Crowds leaned in when he played.
Grown men recorded him on their phones.
Kids asked for high fives after the game.
Parents whispered his name in hallways as if he were already a star.

He did not know what fame was.
He only knew the feeling of being noticed.

Attention became applause.
Applause became identity.

This was the beginning of the glitz.
Not the glamorous kind adults chase.
The childlike version that tells a ten-year-old he is important.

The First Call

His mother answered the phone one evening and heard a coach from across the city ask if her son could join a travel team.
He promised exposure.
He promised development.
He promised that this was how scholarships were earned.

No one mentioned the cost.
The hotels.
The flights.
The uniforms.
The camps.

The private trainers.
The tournament fees.

Youth sports in America had become a marketplace.
Families were the ones paying to keep it alive.

By the time a child reached middle school, the dream of reaching the next level was already attached to a financial burden.
Sports were supposed to lift families out.
In reality, families spent thousands before a single dollar ever flowed back.

What the family paid for with sacrifice, he experienced as privilege.

While his mother worked overtime to cover fees, he was treated like a rising star.

The financial burden fell on the household.

The special treatment fell on him.

This is how the pipeline works.

It rewards the child while it drains the family.

When Privilege Becomes a Lesson

He began to notice small things.
He never carried his own bag.
Adults handled travel details for him.

Meals were paid for.
Mistakes were excused because talent covered everything.
If he was late, they waited.
If he was wrong, they corrected gently.
If he was frustrated, they reassured him he was special.

He did not learn responsibility.
He learned immunity.

He learned that being exceptional meant the rules were optional.

Circuits

He joined an AAU team at eleven.
The circuits were massive and noisy.
Bright banners.
Corporate logos.
Hundreds of teams from multiple states.
Courts lined up side by side like assembly lines.

Shoe companies funded the top circuits.
Nike.
Adidas.
Under Armour.
Brands that built billion-dollar empires now invested in children because the earlier they entered the pipeline, the more influence they gained over the future stars of the sport.

Youth sports spending in the United States had climbed into the tens of billions.
Travel basketball alone had become a multibillion-dollar global machine.
Parents spent an average of $5,000 to $12,000 per year on youth sports.
Some spent far more.
Every year, the industry grew.

A select few kids received free shoes and bags.
For the rest, the cost of being part of the dream was paid in full by parents who believed this was the only path to a better life.

The Arrogance That Forms Quietly

He started noticing how people treated him.
Kids moved aside when he walked through hallways.
Coaches smiled wider when he entered the gym.
Adults bragged about knowing him.

He mistook all of this for value.
He began to believe he was different.

Confidence is healthy.
His confidence began to drift into something else.

Arrogance grows easily when a child is praised more than he is challenged.

He did not choose arrogance.
The environment built it for him.

Eyes Everywhere

At twelve years old, he learned that adults watched him differently.
Not as a child.
As potential.

A highlight video of him dribbling through traffic appeared on YouTube.
Someone created a ranking list for players his age.
Websites tracked his development as if he were a stock.

He still played for fun.
Everyone else played for the future.

Coaches invited him to elite camps that cost more than his mother's rent.
He did not understand what the word elite meant.
He only understood that the shirts were nicer and the courts were cleaner.

He thought they noticed his discipline.
They noticed his marketability.

Too Good for Real Life

He began to believe that jobs were for people without talent.
Homework was for kids who did not have a future.
Responsibilities were for people who were not chosen.

No one corrected him.
No one wanted to disrupt the dream.

Families did not push him toward real skills because they believed he would never need them.
Communities protected him from consequences because he represented hope.

He was not raised to be prepared.
He was raised to be special.

The Market

By thirteen, he was familiar with flights, hotel lobbies, rental vans, and unfamiliar gyms in unfamiliar cities.
He was also familiar with pressure.

He saw kids cry after losses.
Not because of competition, but because they feared disappointing the adults who had invested in them.

Some parents yelled.
Some coaches whispered.
Some trainers promised that the right camp, the

right tournament, or the right circuit could change everything.

They were selling hope.
Hope cost more each year.

The market around him grew faster than his body.
Tournaments expanded.
Fees increased.
Recruiting services multiplied.
Highlight channels profited from content built on the backs of children.

He still thought all of this was normal.

The Gathering Crowd

By fourteen, college coaches knew his name.
Some had watched him play in person.
Some had received grainy footage of his early tournaments.
Some followed the algorithms that tracked every high-performing kid in the region.

He started to believe he was special.
He did not realize that being special was part of what the system needed him to believe.

Every circuit needs stars.
Every camp needs headliners.
Every brand needs the next face of the future.

He was a child.
To them, he was the beginning of a potential business relationship.

The Better Life at a Quiet Price

He lived better than most kids his age.
He wore sponsored gear.
He traveled across states.
He stayed in hotels with indoor pools.
He ate at restaurants he could not pronounce.

But he traded something for all of it.

He traded childhood.
He traded innocence.
He traded the skills he would one day need.
He traded the structure that keeps young men grounded.
He traded the humility that anchors adulthood.

He was given comfort instead of character.
Access instead of understanding.
Exposure instead of education.

The Quiet Shift

The louder the gyms became, the quieter the classrooms felt.

Homework disappeared under the weight of travel.
Teachers excused absences because talent was treated as destiny.
His schedule was dictated by tournaments, not textbooks.

The pipeline he entered had no academic exit.
Everything pointed toward a deeper investment in the same dream.

He believed they were building him up.
In reality, they were narrowing his life.

The Realization That Never Came

At fifteen, he received his first letter from a college program.
He held it like a trophy.
His family celebrated.
The community cheered.

No one realized that the recruiting began years earlier.
Before the letters.
Before the scholarships.
Before the attention.

The system had already decided what he was allowed to become.

He thought the journey began now.
The truth was that it began the moment someone

pointed at him at ten years old and saw something they could shape.

He never questioned when the dream became a pipeline.
He never asked when the game stopped being a game.

He only knew he was chosen.
He did not know he had been measured.

Closing Line

He was recruited for his talent long before he was ever taught the truth.

CHAPTER 2: THE EDUCATIONAL ILLUSION

He arrived at school each morning like every other kid, backpack hanging off one shoulder, homework forgotten somewhere between tournaments and hotel rooms.

Teachers smiled when he walked in.
Not because he was an exceptional student.
Because he was an asset.

They did not know his GPA.
They knew his stat line.

It started subtly.
A teacher letting him retake a quiz he never studied for.
A counselor shifting his schedule to "make things easier."
An administrator pulling him aside to say, "We just want you to stay eligible."

Eligibility mattered more than education.
Winning mattered more than learning.
The future they imagined for him existed far from any classroom.

He was physically present in school.
Academically, he lived somewhere else.

No one said it out loud, but everyone participated in the illusion.
He did not attend class to learn.
He attended class to remain available.

His classmates treated him like a celebrity long before he understood what that meant.
Kids asked for pictures after big games.
Friends posted clips of him dunking in warmups.
Local pages uploaded highlights with captions like "Future star."
Coaches shared his stats on social media before he even got home.

This was the new age of talent.
Before he was ever paid, he was made public.

He started to gain followers he did not know.
Strangers commented under his videos like they were scouting him.
He was tagged in posts from people he had never spoken to.

He grew up in a world where a child could go viral between classes.

He did not realize it yet, but this was the early form of NIL, the unofficial version that shaped him long before the law ever caught up.
He was learning to live in front of an audience.
He was learning to perform, not prepare.

He would sit in classrooms, scrolling through notifications under his desk, watching strangers

assign meaning to his life.
He felt important.
He felt seen.
He felt chosen.

The problem was simple.
Attention replaced education.

Assignments were optional.
Deadlines were flexible.
Excuses were accepted.
Absences were forgiven.

Teachers passed him because they didn't want to disrupt the narrative.
Counselors passed him because they feared being the reason the dream fell apart.
Administrators passed him because his success meant something for the school.

He was not set up to learn.
He was set up to stay eligible.

Travel became the priority.
Practice became the requirement.
Study hall became a suggestion no one enforced.

He spent more hours on buses than in classrooms.
More hours in gyms than reading.
More hours being shaped as a player than developed as a person.

He was not unmotivated.
He was unprotected.

Every shortcut given to him academically became a skill he would never build.
He did not learn discipline.
He did not learn time management.
He did not learn how to advocate for himself.
He did not learn how to plan.
He did not learn how to recover from failure.

He learned instead that adults would fix things for him.
That talent erased responsibility.
That systems would bend to keep him on the court.
That education was an accessory.
That he did not need to learn anything he could not dribble past.

Some kids in school discovered their strengths.
He discovered his usefulness.

Not as a student.
As a symbol.

People loved what he represented.
Few cared whether he grew beyond it.

He could feel eyes on him in the hallways, but they were not the eyes of classmates.
They were spectators.
Fans.
Investors.

Every compliment came with expectation.
Every smile came with pressure.

Every adult saw him as a future headline or a future scholarship announcement.

He was being pushed higher in a system that never asked whether he was growing.

He became isolated inside the attention.
Not lonely.
Just alone in a role no one prepared him for.

He was treated as if he already made it.
He lived as if he already arrived.
He believed the future was guaranteed because everyone around him behaved like it was.

By the time he reached high school, he had already lost more academically than he ever gained athletically.

The system was building a star.
It was not building a man.

He would one day face the world without the skills he was promised school would teach him.
He would one day manage money without learning how to manage himself.
He would one day chase stability without ever learning structure.

No one meant to harm him.
They simply meant to help him win.

And help became the harm.

He was the pride of the school.
The face of the team.
The reason stands filled.

But he was not being educated.
He was being positioned.

He spent more hours on buses than in classrooms,
and everyone called it preparation.

CHAPTER 3: THE NIL ERA: Freedom or a New Trap?

The New Money Before the Old Lessons

They called it freedom.
They called it progress.
They called it empowerment.

For the first time in history, teenagers could make money from their names.
High school stars signed endorsement deals.
College freshmen negotiated contracts like free agents.
Brands chased attention the way scouts used to chase talent.

People celebrated it as long overdue.
But no one stopped to ask the most important question.

If adults with full support systems still struggle to navigate wealth...
what chance does a teenager have with none of the preparation?

NIL did not create opportunity.
It sped up the timeline.
It turned childhood into a marketplace.

It handed money to kids before they ever learned the rules of money.

This was not the beginning of freedom.
It was the acceleration of exposure.

NIL is better than the era when universities made millions while athletes made nothing.

But progress without protection is not progress.

NIL moved the money without moving the guardrails. It gave young athletes revenue without giving them the structure, education, or oversight required to keep them safe. The system corrected yesterday's problem by creating a new one that is just as dangerous.

The Floodgates Open

Before NIL, a teenager had one layer of protection: he could not legally make money from his name.

Now, a 16-year-old can:

- sign contracts
- hire agents (with no oversight)
- negotiate deals
- manage public image
- become a brand ambassador
- owe taxes
- owe deliverables

· owe appearances
· owe social content
· owe adult responsibilities he does not understand

He steps into a world where adults have legal leverage over him,
but he has no financial language, no negotiation literacy, no protection, and no power.

Brands do not sign players.
Brands sign attention.
And teenagers have become the cheapest attention money can buy.

To a company, a 17-year-old with 300k followers is a bargain.
To that teenager, it feels like a blessing.

But every blessing in a capitalist system comes with fine print.

The Predatory Arena

NIL opened the door for:

· agents
· marketing firms
· financial advisors
· brand reps
· talent managers
· contracts written in legal traps
· companies testing the boundaries of exploitation

Before NIL, predators waited until draft night.
Now they wait at orientation.

Before NIL, agents courted juniors and seniors.
Now they court freshmen and sophomores.

Before NIL, families had two years to prepare.
Now families have two weeks.

The rise of NIL created a new kind of agent — one who specializes in quick contracts, viral marketing, and short-term profits.

Players sign without reading.
Parents approve without understanding.
Schools celebrate without questioning.

Everyone gets paid except the person learning how fragile these deals really are.

He Becomes a Business Before He Becomes a Man

NIL tells teenagers:

- build a brand
- monetize your likeness
- grow your platform
- become marketable
- act professional
- behave like a star
- manage your public image
- avoid mistakes because mistakes cost money now

Imagine being 16 and having to think:

"If I say the wrong thing, I might lose my deal."

Imagine being 17 and having to decide:

"Do I trust this adult with my money?"
"What happens if the contract goes bad?"
"What's my tax liability?"
"What does breach of deliverables mean?"

They never learned:

- how to study
- how to manage time
- how to handle pressure
- how to set boundaries
- how to say no
- how to protect themselves
- how to understand financial systems
- how to negotiate

But now they're expected to run a brand.

They were children yesterday.
Today they are businesses.

Businesses with no CFO, no training, no legal team, and no buffer.

Money Arrives Before Maturity

This is where NIL becomes dangerous.

Teenagers do not understand:

· taxes
· liability
· contract structure
· long-term planning
· leverage
· financial predators
· lifestyle inflation
· asset protection
· public fallout
· reputation markets

Brands do.

Agents do.

Advisors do.

Scammers do.

The people entering their lives because of NIL understand the value of attention far better than the kids generating it.

And that imbalance is where the trap lives.

Followers Become a Currency

NIL merged sports and influencer culture into one ecosystem.

A teenager's value is now:

- performance
- personality
- virality
- follower count
- engagement metrics
- marketability
- algorithm behavior

This is not athletic development.
This is digital exploitation.

Teenagers now compete not only on the field
but on timelines, explore pages, and FYP feeds.

Their worth is recalculated daily.

The more visible they become,
the more people feel entitled to access their lives.

The more marketable they become,
the more adults show up with opportunities
disguised as traps.

The more money they make,
the more everyone around them assumes they're
already successful.

But NIL money is rarely life-changing money.

NIL is starter money.
NIL is exposure money.
NIL is temporary money.
NIL is inconsistent money.

And inconsistent money creates consistent instability.

Families Celebrate Before They Understand the Cost

Parents see checks.
They don't see:

- tax audits
- contract obligations
- legal loopholes
- income volatility
- brand control clauses
- mental health strain
- increased visibility = increased danger

Families believe NIL is freedom.

In reality, NIL is the first step into a system that has swallowed grown men whole.

If a 27-year-old with professional protection can blow $40 million...
what chance does a kid have with $40,000 and no protection at all?

The math is simple.
The system is not.

The Illusion of Ownership

NIL makes young athletes feel like they own:

- their image
- their value
- their audience
- their opportunities
- their future

But NIL money is not wealth.
It is not stability.
It is not security.

It is revenue without responsibility.
It is income without structure.
It is power without preparation.
It is opportunity without understanding.
It is pressure disguised as independence.

NIL creates the illusion of ownership while deepening dependence.

Closing Line

It looks like freedom.
It feels like progress.
But for most young athletes, NIL is just the first contract in a life full of fine print, teaching them too early that money can arrive long before maturity ever does.

CHAPTER 4: THE EXPLOSION, NOT THE CLIMB

The Day Everything Changes

The average professional does not rise gradually.
He does not build slowly.
He does not ease into wealth.

He explodes into it.

One signature.
One handshake.
One press conference.
One name across a ticker on draft night.

The world calls it success.
It feels more like velocity.

The cameras capture the moment his life changes.
They never capture the violent transition that follows.

This is not a climb.
It is a launch.
And very few people survive launches without burns.

The Overnight Transformation

He goes from:

• a college apartment to a luxury condo
• dorm food to private chefs
• university trainers to personal performance staff
• borrowed cars to six-figure vehicles
• student crowds to global audiences
• broke classmates to millionaire peers

Nothing in his childhood, his education, or his life prepared him for this acceleration.

One day, he is that kid from the neighborhood.
The next day, he becomes an economic ecosystem.

And everyone wants a piece of the explosion.

The Draft Day Machine

The draft is sold as a celebration.
What people do not realize is that it is also a marketplace.

Behind the hugs, the tears, the glitz, and the optimism, there is a checklist of financial obligations already attached to his name:

• agent cut
• union fees
• taxes
• relocation
• mandatory contributions

· training expenses
· advisor retainers
· family expectations
· housing requirements
· rookie duties
· appearance demands

His contract is not pure income.
It is pre-divided before he ever touches it.

By the time the celebratory smoke clears, the money you think he has is not the money he has.

And that is what most fans never understand.

Welcome to the Infrastructure

The moment a young athlete goes pro, the system assigns him an entire support staff:

· sports agent
· financial advisor
· wealth manager
· accountant
· trainer
· real estate broker
· marketing rep
· brand strategist
· nutritionist
· publicist

These people are not chosen by him.
He has no experience to evaluate them.
He trusts because everyone tells him he should.

And because the explosion is so overwhelming, he hands his life to people who are often more prepared to profit from him than protect him.

Most grown men struggle to vet these roles.
Now imagine being nineteen, too young to legally drink but old enough to be handed a multimillion-dollar ecosystem.

The Money That Disappears Before It Arrives

Here is what the draft night contract does not show:

· signing bonuses taxed at the highest bracket
· agent fees between 1 percent and 4 percent
· advisor fees between 1 percent and 2 percent annually
· mandatory rookie transition programs
· immediate family relocation costs
· lifestyle inflation he did not ask for
· pressure purchases he feels obligated to make
· debt repayment from years of family sacrifice

The number the public sees is not the number in his bank account.
The ground shifts before he ever stands on it.

He went from nothing to wealth in an hour,
but the money itself is already spoken for.

This is the danger of velocity.
It gives the illusion of abundance
before the athlete ever understands sustainability.

The Explosion Creates an Audience

He used to walk down campus hallways unnoticed.
Now he cannot leave his building without someone shouting his name.

He is posted.
He is watched.
He is judged.
He is expected to perform.
He is expected to succeed.
He is expected to give back.
He is expected to stay humble.
He is expected to carry the dream.

Overnight fame is not natural.
Human beings are not built to process attention at this scale.

Childhood did not prepare him.
College did not prepare him.
The system did not prepare him.

They gave him a contract.
They did not give him tools.

The Loneliness of Instant Wealth

There is a moment every young athlete faces after the noise fades.

A night alone in a new condo.
A city he does not know.
A contract he does not understand.
A bank account that feels like a blessing and a threat at the same time.

He realizes no one taught him:

- how to manage wealth
- how to set boundaries
- how to vet advisors
- how to protect his name
- how to handle pressure
- how to say no
- how to lead a life people now expect him to live

The explosion put him on top of the world.
It did not give him the tools to stay there.

The Pressure of Being First

Everyone is proud of him.
Everyone is depending on him.
Everyone says, you made it.

But being first means:

- the family leans on him
- the neighborhood watches him
- the media scrutinizes him
- the peers envy him
- the advisors monetize him

And through all of it, he is still trying to figure out who he is.

He did not get time to grow into himself.
The explosion forced him to play every role at once:

son
savior
brand
business
athlete
provider
public figure

No one in his life carried this kind of pressure.
He has no blueprint to follow.

The Violence of Acceleration

The system teaches the public to believe he should be grateful.

But gratitude does not erase the truth.

The human mind develops slowly.
Wealth arrives instantly.

The explosion creates an emotional and financial disorientation that looks like joy from the outside but feels like survival from the inside.

Velocity has a cost.
And the cost is invisible to everyone except the person living through it.

Closing Line

He did not climb to the top.
He was thrown there.
And the fall that follows is rarely because he failed.
It is because the system celebrated the explosion and never prepared him for the landing.

CHAPTER 5: THE BLACK TAX AT ATHLETE SCALE

He used to think the pressure would ease once he made it.
That was the lie everyone believes before the contract.
The truth is that the weight gets heavier, not lighter, once the money appears.

Back home, the phone never stops ringing.
Not because people are greedy, but because they are hopeful.
They watched him grow.
They prayed for him.
They told their kids about him.
They kept the newspaper clippings on their refrigerators.
They saw his success as a family achievement.
A community achievement.
A generational achievement.

And in many ways, it was.

But the moment he signed the contract, the dream they all shared became a responsibility he now carried alone.

He does not resent them.
He understands them.
He grew up in the same neighborhoods they did.
He knows the struggle they face, the bills that pile up, the emergencies that come without warning.
He knows what it feels like to have no safety net.
He knows what it feels like to be the one everyone pins their hope on.

So when someone says, "Can you help me just this once,"
he cannot say no.
When an uncle says, "It's only a few thousand,"
he cannot refuse.
When a childhood friend says, "I'm trying to start something,"
he feels obligated to listen.
When a parent hints at financial stress,
he feels it in his chest before he ever hears it in their voice.

This is not selfishness from the people around him.
This is survival.
This is history.
This is what happens in families and communities that never had wealth before.

Most Americans feel the Black Tax in small ways.
He feels it at athlete scale.

Everyone believes he has the answers.
Everyone believes he is set for life.

Everyone believes he cannot go broke.
Everyone believes he was chosen to lift them up too.

They do not see what he sees.
They do not see the money leave faster than it arrives.
They do not see the support staff draining his accounts in fees.
They do not see the pressure purchases he makes to keep the peace.
They do not see the lifestyle inflation that follows him everywhere.
They do not see the silent obligations he carries in his heart.

And no one sees the loneliness.

He cannot tell his family no without feeling like he is betraying them.
He cannot tell his boys no without feeling like he left them behind.
He cannot tell the world no without becoming the headline they laugh at.

He becomes the savior and the target at the same time.

He feels guilty for having more.
He feels guilty for not giving more.
He feels guilty for wanting boundaries.
He feels guilty for needing space.

He has spent his entire life fighting to get out, only to realize that success pulled him back in deeper than before.

There is a night every athlete remembers.
A night where he looks at his bank account and realizes he cannot help everybody.
A night where he understands he has become the safety net for people who never had one.
A night where he wonders if he will ever be allowed to grow into a man without being responsible for saving everyone who watched him grow up.

The moment he realizes helping everyone is actually hurting his long-term ability to help anyone.

That is the night he learns the truth about the Black Tax.

It is not a bill.
It is not a number.
It is not a transaction.

It is the emotional weight of being first.
It is the cultural weight of being chosen.
It is the generational weight of being the one who made it.

And at athlete scale, it becomes too heavy for any one person to carry.

He loves his people.
He loves where he came from.
He loves the pride they feel when they see him on

TV.
But he is still learning how to be a man with money in a world that taught him how to survive without any.

He cannot save everyone.
He will try anyway.
That is what makes the burden so heavy.
That is what makes the Black Tax invisible until it is too late.

The world thinks his downfall will come from bad spending.
In reality, it often comes from good intentions.

He is not irresponsible.
He is not reckless.
He is not ungrateful.

He is simply human, carrying a generational weight the world cannot see
and a financial pressure he never had time to understand
while everyone around him believes
that being the first to make it means he must be the first to give it all away.

CHAPTER 6: THE INDUSTRY AROUND HIM

Everyone says the athlete has a team around him.
No one asks who that team actually serves.

The Ecosystem Pretending To Protect Him

Everyone tells him he is surrounded by professionals.
Agents. Advisors. Managers. Publicists. Trainers.
Every one of them claims to be there for his best interest.

But industries do not exist for protection.
Industries exist for profit.

He enters the league believing he has a team.
He does not realize he has walked into an economy.

An economy powered by him.
An economy built around him.
An economy that survives whether he succeeds or collapses.

To the outside world, he has help.
In reality, he has exposure.

Agents: The Gatekeepers and the Sellers

His agent shakes his hand on draft night.
Warm smile. Encouraging words. Strategic promises.

The truth is more complicated.

An agent represents him, yes
but an agent also represents the team
the league
other players
brand interests
and their own agency's bottom line.

Most agents are good at their jobs.
But their job is not to build his life.
Their job is to negotiate a contract and take their percentage.

He believes the agent is his first line of defense.
The agent believes he is a client inside a portfolio.

There is a difference.

Financial Advisors: The Most Dangerous Title in His Circle

This is the role fans never talk about
but it is the one that has destroyed more wealth than poor spending ever has.

Anyone can call themselves a financial advisor.
There is no uniform standard.
No mandatory training.
No guaranteed loyalty.

Some advisors are brilliant.
Some are ethical.
Many are not.

They control access to his accounts.
They recommend investments he does not understand.
They charge fees he never questions.
They position themselves as experts because he has no way to verify.

And when an athlete goes broke,
the world blames the athlete
not the advisor who drained him quietly over eight seasons.

The biggest scandals in athlete history
have almost always involved an advisor
not the athlete himself.

But the media never tells that part of the story.

Managers and Marketing Reps: The Ones Who Monetize His Image

Everyone is excited about his platform.
Brands. Agencies. Media outlets.

They want him to be marketable
which means they want him to be profitable.

To them, he is not a person.
He is a product.
A storyline.
A narrative that can be sold.

They build his public identity
not to protect him
but to monetize him.

They encourage the content
the exposure
the interviews
the appearances
the endorsements

because every spotlight on him
is a revenue stream for them.

No one tells him that attention is a currency
and he is paying the highest price.

The Media: The Machine That Needs a Story, Not a Life

The media follows him everywhere
not because they care
but because he sells.

The miracle sells.
The climb sells.

The contract sells.
The controversy sells.
The collapse sells even more.

The media does not need him to be whole.
It needs him to be interesting.

He thinks they are covering his success.
They are studying their next headline.

They celebrate him before they devour him.
They shape narratives that follow him for years.
They turn mistakes into content.
They turn vulnerability into entertainment.

And when he collapses
they call it inevitable
even though they helped create the pressure that caused it.

The media profits twice
from the rise
and from the fall.

He profits from neither.

Everyone Eats Before He Does

Behind every contract he signs
is a chain of people taking their cut.

Behind every endorsement
is a list of fees.

Behind every appearance
a stack of invoices.

Behind every dollar he makes
is a system already positioned to take its share.

Fans see the income.
The industry sees the opportunity.
He sees the leftovers.

This is not mismanagement.
It is math.
It is the math of an ecosystem that survives by consuming the athlete at its center.

He Walked Into a World With No Neutral Parties

The tragic truth is that he has no purely objective advisors.

His family wants safety.
His friends want access.
His agent wants the next contract.
His advisor wants assets under management.
His manager wants brand growth.
The media wants a story.
The team wants performance.
The fans want entertainment.
The league wants profitability.

Everyone wants something from him.

Almost no one teaches him how to want something for himself
how to build something that lasts
how to protect what he earns
how to grow beyond the game.

He is not irresponsible.
He is outnumbered.

Closing Line

The industry calls him an asset.
The world calls him a hero.
But in the middle of all the hands reaching for him
he is still learning the hardest truth of all.
He was never taught how to be the owner of the life everyone else is benefitting from.

CHAPTER 7: THE PSYCHOLOGY OF VALIDATION SPENDING

He did not start spending to show off.
He started spending to feel normal.

People think athletes waste money because they want attention.
Most of the time, they do it because they want relief.

He spent because he was lonely.
He spent because he was overwhelmed.
He spent because he felt the pressure of being first.
He spent because spending became the easiest way to quiet everything he had never been taught to confront.

No one ever explains the emotional cost of sudden wealth.
People only explain the math.

The math is simple.
The emotions are not.

There is a moment when the applause fades
and the silence becomes louder than any crowd he has ever played for.
He is alone with a version of himself he never had space to meet.

The car makes him feel like he belongs.
The jewelry makes him feel like he deserves to be here.
The clothes make him feel like he fits the image.
The dinners make him feel generous, important, connected.
The trips make him feel free.

None of it is arrogance.
It is survival.
It is the psychology of a young man trying to soothe the parts of himself the world never cared to understand.

When you grow up with less, you learn early that things carry meaning.
New shoes were confidence.
A clean outfit was pride.
A gift was gratitude.
A meal out was celebration.

He brought those meanings with him into wealth.

Only this time, the numbers changed.
The emotions did not.

He remembers the first big purchase.
Not the price
but the feeling.
For a moment, everything made sense.
He felt powerful.
He felt worthy.

He felt like he had finally caught up to the life everyone told him he deserved.

No one teaches young athletes that money cannot protect them from themselves.
No one explains how childhood wounds follow you into adulthood.
No one warns them that validation is the most expensive emotion a person can feed.

He spent to reward himself.
He spent to silence doubt.
He spent to avoid the conversations he never wanted to have.
He spent to look like the version of success the world demanded from him.

Every time someone said
"You're the man,"
he felt the pressure to prove it again.

Every time someone said
"You're rich now,"
he felt obligated to act like it.

Every time someone said
"Put us on,"
he felt guilt for wanting distance.

He built an identity around meeting expectations that were never his to carry.

And the crazy part is this.
Most of his spending was not even for him.

It was for the people around him.
To keep the peace.
To keep the image.
To keep the love.
To keep the access.
To keep the version of himself that made everyone else comfortable.

Validation spending does not look reckless in the moment.
It looks necessary.
It looks like belonging.
It looks like relief.

It is only later, when the career slows down, or the money thins out,
that he realizes how much of his spending
was an attempt to fill the emotional gaps he never learned how to name.

He never wanted to be flashy.
He wanted to feel whole.

Money gave him the ability to touch wholeness
but never hold it.

The world told him to be humble.
The league told him to be professional.
The family told him to be grateful.
The fans told him to be legendary.

No one told him how to be human.

Validation spending is not about overspending.
It is about trying to find pieces of yourself in the places wealth gives you access to.
It is about chasing the feeling the spotlight gave you
when the spotlight is no longer there.

It is about surviving emotions you were never taught to feel
with money you were never taught to manage.

He never stood a chance.
Not because he failed
but because the world celebrated his talent
and ignored his heart.

The world thinks athletes spend because they want more.
In truth
they spend because they want something money cannot buy.

Peace.
Identity.
Acceptance.
Belonging.
Freedom from being first.
Freedom from being responsible for everyone else.
Freedom from the expectations that wrapped around them the moment they became somebody.

He is not irresponsible.
He is not wasteful.
He is not reckless.

He is a young man trying to solve emotional problems with financial tools
because no one ever taught him the tools he actually needed.

He does not need more discipline.
He needs more understanding.
He needs more guidance.
He needs more space to grow into himself.
He needs a world that sees him as a person before it sees him as a paycheck.

Until that happens
validation spending will always be the quiet leak
in the life of young men who were handed everything
before they ever had the chance to know themselves.

CHAPTER 8: THE TRAPS NO ONE TALKS ABOUT

The world thinks the biggest threats to an athlete's money are cars, jewelry, houses, or bad investments.

It is rarely those things.

The most dangerous traps are the ones that do not look like traps at all.
The ones that arrive quietly, wrapped in attention, admiration, validation, or desire.
The ones that do not ask for money at first.
The ones that feel good in the moment.
The ones he does not see coming because nobody ever warned him.

When he becomes somebody, he does not just gain fans.
He gains access.
More access than any young man has ever been prepared to manage.

Sudden access is a form of wealth.
And like every form of wealth, it comes with predators.

He is visible now.
He is desirable now.
He is valuable now.
He is financially attractive now.

He is emotionally useful now.
He is an opportunity now.

There are people who do not want him.
They want what being close to him provides.

And because he is young
because he is lonely
because he is overwhelmed
because he is still trying to grow into the man the world thinks he already is
he often mistakes attention for connection.

No one teaches him how to tell the difference.

He is not arrogant for wanting affection.
He is human for wanting to be seen.

The problem is that fame creates a distortion.
People act differently around him.
Relationships form faster than they should.
Promises feel deeper than they are.
Intentions are hidden under charm.
Emotions are confused with opportunity.
And he confuses access with intimacy.

Some people approach him with genuine interest.
Some approach with plans.
Some approach with resentment.
Some approach with strategies.
Some approach with the belief that his success is something they can claim for themselves.

He has no experience to navigate this.
He has no mentor for this.
He has no preparation for this.

So he learns through mistakes.
Expensive mistakes.
Public mistakes.
Lifetime mistakes.

Not because he lacks intelligence
but because he lacks exposure.

A young man who never learned emotional boundaries
cannot build them overnight
while standing in the brightest spotlight of his life.

He was never taught how to choose people.
He was never taught how to protect himself in relationships.
He was never taught how to evaluate intentions.
He was never taught how to walk away.
He was never taught how to be desired without being devoured.

He experiences love the same way he experiences money.
Suddenly.
Intensely.
Without warning.
Without guidance.
Without the gradual development, most people get to grow through.

So he learns the hard way that:

attention is not affection
desire is not care
consistency is not loyalty
intimacy is not trust
and access is not love

He learns that being chosen for who he is publicly does not mean being valued for who he is privately.

He learns that some people enter his life
not to build with him
but to build from him.

He learns that vulnerability is expensive.
That mistakes can cost millions.
That romantic decisions can become legal decisions.
That emotional confusion can become financial collapse.
That trust can become a headline.

He learns that there are people who see him as an exit plan.
People who study him the way scouts study film.
People who know exactly what to say.
People who understand how to position themselves.
People who have played this game longer than he has been alive.

He learns that the world is full of people who want pieces of him
but not the whole of him.

And in the quiet moments between games and appearances
he realizes something even heavier.

He is looking for connection in a world that treats him like a transaction.

He is searching for sincerity in environments built on performance.
He is hoping for trust in rooms full of agendas.
He is trying to build stability on ground that shifts every time he breathes.

Most people will call this part of the story recklessness.
It is not recklessness.
It is emotional adolescence happening in adulthood after a childhood spent being groomed for performance instead of relationships.

He was trained to compete
but never trained to connect.

He was prepared to win
but never prepared to choose the right people to win with.

That is the trap no one talks about.

The trap of becoming a man before learning how to be one.
The trap of loneliness with access.
The trap of affection without clarity.
The trap of desire without protection.
The trap of love influenced by leverage.
The trap of building relationships in the dark
while the world watches him every day in the light.

He does not need shame.
He needs guidance.
He needs mentors.
He needs truth tellers who are not on his payroll.
He needs people who see him as a person
not as a platform.

Until he has that
he will continue to walk into the same emotional traps
that have cost athletes more money and peace
than any purchase ever could.

The world thinks athletes fall because they spend too much.
They rarely realize the truth.

The most expensive decisions he will ever make
are the ones he makes with his heart
not his wallet.

CHAPTER 9: THE DRAFT-DAY MACHINE

The Day That Looks Like Freedom

Draft day is marketed as liberation.
A young man walks across a stage, shakes a commissioner's hand, puts on a hat, and smiles for the camera.

Everyone watching sees a dream fulfilled.

No one sees the system that has been preparing to profit from him long before the cameras turned on.

Draft day is not the beginning of his career.
It is the beginning of the machine taking ownership.

The Moment the Pick Is Announced

The world sees celebration.
Behind the scenes, corporate gears start turning.

Agents renegotiate their cut.
Financial advisors prepare paperwork they began drafting weeks ago.
Marketing firms position him as a brand asset.
Apparel companies line up endorsement tiers.
Team executives discuss how to maximize his value.

Media outlets prewrite narratives.
Social platforms explode with commentary.

It feels like everyone is cheering for him.
In reality, everyone is calculating what he is worth.

Draft day is not a victory.
It is an acquisition.

The Prebuilt Narrative

Before he even steps on the stage, the storyline is set.

He saved his family.
He is the next big thing.
He is ready to be a star.

These stories are not for him.
They are for the machine.

Narratives sell jerseys.
Narratives drive engagement.
Narratives create pressure.
Narratives lock him into an identity he did not choose.

Once the story is written, he must now live up to it at any cost.

Who Draft Day Really Serves

The team gets a promising asset.
The league gets a fresh storyline.
The media gets a new face to monetize.
Corporations get an influencer who comes prepackaged with millions of followers.
Colleges get proof their program builds pros.
The NCAA gets validation of its talent pipeline.
Sponsors get someone who moves product.
Agents and advisors get long-term clients.

Everyone eats.

Except him.

He gets money, yes.
But most of that money is already spoken for.

Draft day is the moment the world shifts from cheering for him to feeding from him.

The Instant Pressure to Lead

Before he even cashes his first check:

Family asks for help.
Friends expect opportunities.
Old coaches seek recognition.
Communities claim him.
Organizations market him.
Reporters scrutinize him.
Strangers judge him.

He becomes a symbol before he becomes a man.

Draft day does not prepare him for pressure.
Draft day creates the pressure.

The Hidden Costs Embedded in the Celebration

The suit he wore today was styled by someone on a retainer.
The draft preparation involved trainers, nutritionists, and specialists.
The advisors and lawyers are already billing.
The relocations, housing, and transportation fall on him.
The agent's percentage is baked into every incoming check.
The media expectations are immediate.
The corporate appearances are mandatory.

The moment he is drafted, he becomes responsible for an entire economic ecosystem.

The Isolation No One Sees

Draft day looks crowded.
Draft day feels alone.

He smiles for cameras that will forget him in twenty-four hours if he does not perform.
He stands on a stage built to elevate him but ultimately designed to spotlight his every mistake.

He enters a league where the average career lasts only a few years.
He signs contracts that look enormous until everyone takes their piece.

And he steps into a life he was never prepared for.

Money without financial literacy.
Fame without emotional maturity.
Responsibility without guidance.
Expectations without stability.

Draft day is the entrance to the machine, not the escape from it.

The Machine Knows He Is Replaceable

Teams swap players.
Media cycles rotate.
Corporations move on.
Fans shift to the next highlight.

His value is temporary.
The machine's hunger is permanent.

He is not drafted for his future.
He is drafted for his usefulness.

The moment he stops performing, the machine does not break.
It replaces him.

The Quiet Truth About Draft Day

Draft day does not mark the day he made it.

It marks the day he becomes responsible for keeping everyone else's money flowing.

Draft day is the most celebrated moment of his life and the least understood.

The world sees a young man entering wealth.
In reality, a young man is entering a system designed to consume him.

He stands on that stage thinking he finally owns something.
The quiet truth is that the system now owns him.

The Line That Defines This Chapter

Everyone sees draft day as the moment he becomes the center of the world.
No one sees that it is also the day he stops being seen as a person
and starts being seen as a product.

CHAPTER 10: THE CONTRACT EVERYONE EATS FROM

The Headline Number Is a Performance

When the contract is announced, the world hears one number.

Four years. Eighty million.
Five years. One hundred twenty million.
Guaranteed. Incentives. Bonuses. Options.

The headline becomes the identity.
It becomes the expectation.
It becomes the myth.

People see the number.
No one sees the truth behind it.
The contract the world praises is not the contract he actually receives.
It is a marketing tool for the league, the team, and the agent.

The contract he signs is not the same contract the world celebrates.

The First Cuts Come Immediately

Before he touches a dollar:

- Agent takes a percentage
- Financial advisor charges a fee
- Lawyer bills for contract review
- Accountant prepares for tax structuring
- Team withholds state and federal taxes
- Union fees come out
- Insurance and benefits are deducted

By the time the dust settles, the real number is often less than half of what the world believes he earned.

His eighty million is really thirty-five.
His one hundred twenty million is really forty-five.

The public will judge him on the number he never touched.

The Contract Is Built to Protect the Team, Not the Player

Teams design contracts around their needs, not his security.

- Non-guaranteed years
- Team options disguised as stability
- Performance bonuses tied to unrealistic thresholds
- Injury clauses that shift the risk entirely onto him
- Offset language that limits future earning protection

The contract is not a promise.
It is a permission slip.

They can cut him at any time.
They can trade him without warning.
They can void guarantees if circumstances break their way.
They hold the advantage at every line of the agreement.

He signs, believing he is protected.
They sign, knowing they are protected.

Everyone Has a Percentage Except Him

The modern athlete is not a solo act.
He is a corporation with moving parts, personalities, and payroll obligations.

Every check activates a chain reaction:

Agent: 2 to 4 percent
Manager: 10 percent
Financial advisor: 1 percent every year
Private trainers: monthly or seasonal fees
Chef and nutritionist: weekly fees
Security: hourly or salaried
Brand manager: retainer or percentage
Publicist: retainer
Tax accountant: quarterly fees

He is a young man supporting full-time adults.

The world jokes about him having an entourage.
They never consider that some of the entourage wears suits.

State Taxes Change Everything

If he plays in a state with a high tax rate, his earnings drop instantly.

California takes over thirteen percent.
New York takes nearly eleven.
Even away games trigger "jock taxes" that charge him based on where he performs.

He earns money in multiple states and owes money to every one of them.

By the time he pays tax obligations, the number the world thinks he pocketed is a fraction of reality.

The contract headline is a fantasy.
The tax structure is the truth.

The Inflation of Expectations

His friends and family do not expect him to live on the net number.
They expect him to live on the headline.

They expect:

- cars
- houses
- trips
- loans
- bailouts
- investments

· sponsorships
· generosity without limits

No one adjusts their expectations to his net income. Everyone adjusts their expectations to the number announced on ESPN.

He becomes responsible for lifestyles based on money he never received.

The Contract Is an Ecosystem

A contract is not a document.
It is a structure that feeds people.

Agents build reputation.
Teams sell hope.
Media builds narratives.
Corporations build campaigns.
Colleges build recruiting pitches.
Financial firms build client portfolios.
Leagues build storylines.

The athlete builds the least.
He holds the most risk.

Guaranteed Money Is Not What It Seems

Even guaranteed money has conditions.

If he is injured, waived, traded, or fails to meet vague clauses about conduct or performance, teams can delay, reduce, or restructure payouts.

Guaranteed is not guaranteed.
It is conditional security disguised as certainty.

He cannot walk away from the contract.
The team can.

The Real Financial Timeline

The world thinks the contract secures his future for life.
In reality, it secures his bills for a few years.

Most athletes sign their biggest contract at twenty-two or twenty-three.
Their peak earning window ends before age thirty.
Their career is shorter than their financial responsibilities.
Their income ends before their identity matures.
Their earning power collapses before their learning curve begins.

He is expected to build generational wealth
under financial conditions that barely allow him to build personal stability.

The Line That Defines This Chapter

The world thinks the contract makes him rich.
The truth is that the contract makes everyone around him rich

and leaves him with the responsibility of surviving the leftovers.

CHAPTER 11: THE CAREER CLIFF

He spent his entire life climbing toward one moment.
He never realized how fast the climb would end.

There is a day in every athlete's life when the income stops.
It does not stop gently.
It stops like a door that closes and does not open again.

He does not know which game is his last.
He does not know which injury is the difference between recovery and release.
He does not know which season is the final one the machine will tolerate.
He only knows that one morning, he wakes up and the career he built everything around is no longer his.

The world thinks he is prepared for this.
He is not.

He is twenty-seven.
Sometimes twenty-five.
Sometimes nineteen.
He cannot even legally drink in some states when the machine decides he is replaceable.

People talk about the average career length like it is a statistic.
For him, it is a countdown he never saw ticking.

Three years in the NFL.
Four years in the NBA.
Two years on a rookie deal.
One injury.
One trade.
One misstep.
One draft class behind him, that is younger, cheaper, and free of injury history.

The machine is always looking for the next value.
Not the next man.

The check stops before the identity forms.
The money ends before the maturity begins.
The earning power evaporates before the financial literacy settles in.

He prepared for games.
He prepared for pressure.
He prepared for the spotlight.
He did not prepare for silence.

The silence after a career is heavier than any arena he ever played in.

He wakes up with the same body that once made him valuable.
Now it is a cost.
Knees aching.
Back tight.

Ankles stiff.
Years of impact waiting to be felt fully for the first time.

He thought retirement would feel like freedom.
It feels like loss.

Loss of identity.
Loss of purpose.
Loss of structure.
Loss of routine.
Loss of the only world that ever made sense to him.

He was praised for what he could do physically.
Now he is left with what he must face emotionally.

The world assumes he is rich.
The world assumes he is stable.
The world assumes he is prepared.
The world assumes the contract guaranteed a lifetime of comfort.

The world is wrong.

The moment the income stops, the expenses do not.
The responsibilities do not.
The family expectations do not.
The lifestyle pressure does not.
The emotional needs do not.
The financial commitments he made in good faith do not.

Everything he built on the illusion of future earnings now hangs from a thread.

He begins to realize what the machine already knew.
His career was never designed to last.
The system was designed to replace him long before he reached stability.

The cliff is not the end of a career.
The cliff is the beginning of the consequences.

He tries coaching.
He tries training kids.
He tries speaking.
He tries business ventures he does not understand.
He tries to maintain the image people still expect from him.
He tries to figure out what his life looks like without the only thing he ever mastered.

He has to rebuild while the world believes he is already built.

He is not a millionaire learning how to stay rich.
He is a young man learning how to start over.
He is a first-generation earner who did not get a second-generation runway.
He is the provider still trying to provide with a shrinking set of tools.

This is the part the world never sees.

The cliff is not dramatic.
It is quiet.
It is slow.
It is humiliating in ways he never admits.
It is lonely in ways he does not have language for.
It is frightening in ways he never imagined when he was fifteen with college scouts in the stands.

He realized this truth too late.

The career gave him money.
It did not give him time.
It did not give him skills.
It did not give him mentorship.
It did not give him stability.
It did not give him the blueprint he needed to survive after the lights went off.

He was built for the spotlight.
He was never taught what to do once he walked out of it.

He stood on a cliff that everyone knew existed except him.

The fans knew.
The teams knew.
The agents knew.
The league knew.
The machine knew.

He was the only one who thought the ground beneath him was solid.

The quiet truth is this.

He is not falling because he made mistakes.
He is falling because the system was never designed to hold him up once he was no longer useful.

The world sees the cliff as failure.
In reality, the cliff is the design.

He spent his youth building a career.
Now he must spend his adulthood building a life.

This is the moment athletes discover what the machine never tells them.

The applause was temporary.
The risk was permanent.
And the contract that once felt life-changing stopped changing the moment the career did.

The curve ends here for most of them.
Not in luxury.
Not in scandal.
Not in shame.

It ends in a quiet, terrifying truth.

He was prepared to play.
He was never prepared to be done.

CHAPTER 12: THE PSYCHOLOGY OF LEAGUES AND OWNERS

The System Was Never Built for Them

People think leagues are sports organizations.
They are financial ecosystems.
Entertainment machines.
Revenue engines.

The athletes provide the skill.
The owners control the structure.
The league protects the structure.

From the moment he enters the draft pool, he is not entering a sport.
He is entering a business model that existed long before he was born and will continue long after he is gone.

The rules were written without him in mind.
The rules were written to keep the system stable.
The rules were written to ensure the machine always wins.

Owners Do Not Bet on Players. Owners Bet on Predictability

Owners are not emotional.
They are not invested in individual lives.
They are invested in:

- revenue
- predictability
- performance windows
- asset management
- public relations
- league stability
- long-term financial control

Owners do not view an athlete as a partner.
They view him as a risk profile.

How fast he runs.
How durable his body is.
How much value he adds.
How long he will last.
How easily he can be replaced.

This is not cruelty.
It is the psychology of investment.

And he is the investment.

The Combine Is A Marketplace, Not An Evaluation

This is why the combine exists.
People call it an evaluation.
Owners treat it like a marketplace.

He is weighed.
Measured.
Timed.
Scheduled.
Interviewed.
Ranked.
Converted into metrics that can be placed into financial models.

A teenager becomes data.
A young man becomes a projection.
A human becomes a risk profile.

The combine looks like an athletic event.
It functions like an auction where no one uses the word.

The public sees excitement.
The owners see liability scores.
The scouts see potential.
The economists see depreciation curves.

This is the first moment he learns, without anyone saying it, that the league understands him far better than he understands the league.

The Machine Protects Ownership, Not Labor

In every professional league, the underlying principle is simple.

Owners hold power.
Labor is interchangeable.

Salary caps protect ownership.
Draft order protects ownership.
Rookie contracts protect ownership.
Trade rules protect ownership.
Guaranteed money loopholes protect ownership.
Franchise tags protect ownership.
Collective bargaining limitations protect ownership.

Every structural component exists to maintain balance for the billionaires, not the players.

The athlete enters the league believing he has made it.
The league sees him as someone the system must keep in place.

Not elevated.
Not empowered.
Not equal.
Contained.

Talent Is Celebrated. Leverage Is Controlled

Teams will praise his skill.
They will promote his personality.
They will highlight his branding potential.

As long as he does not disrupt the hierarchy.

Any sign of leverage is neutralized quickly.

If he negotiates aggressively, he is labeled difficult.
If he challenges a coach, he is labeled uncoachable.
If he asks for more, he is labeled entitled.
If he thinks independently, he is labeled a distraction.

The league loves stars.
The league does not love stars who understand power.

There is an unspoken rule.

Be great.
Do not be disruptive.
Perform.
Do not challenge the structure that profits from your performance.

The Draft Is the First Control Mechanism

College players do not choose their employers.
Employers choose them.

He cannot negotiate location.
He cannot negotiate terms beyond rookie scale.
He cannot choose a system that develops his skill.
He cannot choose a culture that fits who he is.

He is locked in before he ever steps on the court or field.

This is not a meritocracy.
It is a labor draft designed to distribute talent in a way that maintains the league's financial balance sheet.

He is told draft day is a celebration.
The league sees it as allocation.

The Salary Cap Protects the Machine, Not the Athlete

The cap is designed so that teams can never lose control.

It limits what players can earn.
It limits how contracts are structured.
It limits the length of deals.
It limits player mobility.
It limits negotiation power.
It limits how far an athlete can rise financially before the system reins him back in.

Fans think the salary cap creates fairness.
In reality, it creates cost certainty for billionaires.

Certainty is the most important psychological need of ownership.

Players create highlights.
Owners create rules.

The Short Career Window Is Not an Accident

Every league benefits from fast turnover.

Younger bodies cost less.
Younger athletes have fewer demands.
Younger players accept structure without question.
Younger rosters keep team expenses low.
Younger rookies create fresh narratives for media and marketing.

The machine is designed to celebrate youth and discard the mature.

Older players understand.

They know the business.
They know the system.
They know the leverage points.
They know how to negotiate.
They know their value.

Owners prefer athletes who are grateful, not knowledgeable.

The career cliff is not just physical.
It is structural.

The Illusion of Wealth Keeps the System Quiet

The league depends on one myth.

The myth that athletes are all rich.
Rich enough to complain.
Rich enough to be fine.
Rich enough to endure anything.

As long as the public believes this, no one questions:

· contract structures
· non-guaranteed deals
· the short lifespan of careers
· the lack of financial protection
· the mental health consequences
· the absence of ownership paths

Public perception keeps ownership safe.

The athlete must look wealthy, even when the structure undermines him.

Owners Do Not Fear Losing Players. They Fear Losing Control

As long as players:

· entertain
· generate revenue
· remain replaceable
· do not unionize aggressively
· do not demand equity
· do not challenge media narratives
· do not disrupt the machine

the league remains what it has always been.

Powerful.
Predictable.
Profitable.
Protected.

The moment athletes question the system, the machine reacts.

Quickly.
Quietly.
Collectively.

Control is the primary language of ownership.

The Line That Defines This Chapter

The league does not need him to fail.
The league only needs him to remain manageable.
The entire system is designed with one goal in mind.

Protect the structure.
Not the players who keep it alive.

CHAPTER 13: THE ECONOMICS OF VISIBILITY

Why Fame Pays Everyone Except the Athlete

Visibility feels like value.
But visibility is not value.
It is a commodity the athlete does not own, even when it is built on his name.

He is praised for drawing attention.
He is compensated for drawing crowds.
He is celebrated for generating clicks, views, storylines, debates, and moments.

But the system designed around him monetizes visibility in ways he never touches.

He thinks visibility is a gift.
The system treats visibility as an asset.
An asset he does not control.

This is the trap.

The Attention Economy Was Built on His Back

Every highlight becomes revenue.
Every viral moment becomes content.

Every interview becomes inventory for someone else's business.

Networks profit.
Universities profit.
Agents profit.
Brands profit.
Leagues profit.
Social platforms profit.
Streaming partners profit.

The only person guaranteed nothing is the athlete whose face drives the entire machine.

Visibility is treated like currency.
But he does not get to spend it.
He only gets to supply it.

Fame Has a Financial Shadow

When a star athlete goes viral, the economy surges behind him.

Jersey sales spike.
Merchandise sells out.
Traffic surges on league websites.
Advertisers increase their bids.
Sponsors renegotiate rates.
Networks use the moment in commercial packages.
Analytics teams clip every angle for future profit.

His likeness becomes a brand asset.
His story becomes a marketing funnel.
His face becomes a billboard for a product he does not own.

The athlete sees applause.
The system sees opportunity.
Two different realities tied to one moment.

Social Media Turned Visibility Into a Public Marketplace

Today, visibility is no longer passive.
It is tracked, measured, monetized, packaged, and optimized.

Followers influence draft projections.
Engagement affects endorsement offers.
Algorithms can make or break perceived value.
A 15-second clip can change a career.
A negative storyline can destroy leverage.
A viral dunk can extend opportunity.
A viral mistake can erase it.

He is living inside an attention economy he did not design.
A marketplace where he is the product.
A product that depends on remaining relevant.

Relevance becomes survival.
This is the problem.

NIL Promised Freedom. It Delivered Exposure Dependency.

NIL changed the rules.
But it did not change the power structure.

Teenagers now enter the spotlight years before they enter the league.
They are rewarded for attention, not discipline.
They are measured by reach, not readiness.
They are surrounded by "teams" they did not vet.
They are offered quick money before they understand long-term consequences.

NIL gave athletes revenue.
But it also handed corporations and agents early access to a new generation of unprepared earners.

It is not evil.
But it is not neutral.

For every teenager who builds a foundation, ten become dependent on the very visibility that will later deceive them.

Visibility becomes validation.
Validation becomes currency.
Currency becomes identity.
Identity becomes leverage for the system, not the athlete.

If adults with full support systems still struggle to navigate wealth, what chance does a teenager have with none of the preparation?

Visibility Distorts Value

A star athlete may be told:

"You're worth millions."

But worth to whom?
And paid by whom?

Visibility creates the illusion that he is powerful.
The illusion that fame protects him.
The illusion that influence translates into ownership.

It does not.

Visibility is leverage only when it is backed by:

- legal protection
- financial education
- equity
- long-term contracts
- business literacy
- understanding the curve
- advisors who work for him, not around him
- a strategy beyond the spotlight

Without structure, visibility becomes a liability.

The Hidden Costs of Being Seen

Visibility also amplifies risk.

One misstep becomes a headline.
One mistake becomes a narrative.
One moment becomes a storyline that follows him for years.

Visibility makes him profitable.
Visibility also makes him vulnerable.

Corporations can replace him.
Media can turn on him.
Brands can drop him.
Fans can forget him.
Algorithms can bury him.

Visibility is loud.
Value is quiet.
He was taught to chase the loud part.

Everyone Gets Paid From His Story Except Him

The athlete sees highlight reels.
The system sees revenue streams.

Some athletes start podcasts and believe they finally own their story.

But most podcasts are funded, produced, distributed, and monetized by companies that keep the real equity.

The athlete brings the spotlight.

The network owns the system.

Even in the medium built on his voice, he is still the talent, not the owner.

A single March Madness tournament can generate more than a billion dollars, yet most players leave with debt.

A bowl game appearance can bring millions to a university, yet players see none of it until NIL.

Sneaker companies sign billion-dollar deals with leagues, yet most athletes never see beyond endorsement crumbs.

EA Sports sells millions of video games built on athlete likenesses.
The athletes once received nothing.

Corporate interests have always known one truth:

Athlete visibility is the most underpriced commodity in American sports.

The Visibility Illusion

He thinks being seen is success.
He thinks popularity is progress.
He thinks attention is protection.
He thinks fame guarantees financial survival.

Visibility makes him feel safe.
The economics behind it prove he is not.

The system has spent decades perfecting one strategy:

Profit from the athlete's visibility.
Limit the athlete's ownership of that visibility.

He becomes a global figure without becoming a global earner.

This is the tragedy.
This is the illusion.
This is the mechanism behind the invisible $100 million.

The Line That Defines This Chapter

He believed visibility would secure him.
But visibility only secured everyone around him.

He created the attention.
They collected the revenue.

He supplied the story.
They owned the rights.

Visibility made him famous.
It never made him free.

CHAPTER 14: THE PATH TO BUILDING DIFFERENTLY

The Shift From Lifestyle to Legacy

Most athletes believe wealth begins with the contract.
Real wealth begins with the structure they build around the contract.

A lifestyle is temporary.
A system is permanent.

The difference between the two is the difference between appearing wealthy and staying wealthy.

He has to learn this.
The culture has to learn this.
Anyone trying to break the curve has to learn this.

This is the chapter that separates the dream from the architecture.

The Shift That Changes Everything

At some point, an athlete has to choose which future he is building.

A lifestyle future.
Or a cashflow future.

A lifestyle future lasts as long as the checks.
A cashflow future lasts long after the last whistle.

A lifestyle requires consumption.
A cashflow future requires structure.

A lifestyle collapses without income.
A cashflow future creates income.

He was never taught the difference.
The culture rarely teaches the difference.
The system benefits when he never learns the difference.

Learning the difference is the first step toward building differently.

The Ownership Muscle

He has trained everything except the part of himself that will decide his financial life.

He trains his body.
He trains his skill.
He trains his reflexes.
He trains his endurance.

But the financial mind is a muscle too.

If it is not strengthened, the system will always be stronger.
If it is never trained, he will always react instead of build.
If no one teaches him how ownership works, he will always operate inside someone else's structure.

Ownership is not confidence.
It is literacy.
It is planning.
It is the discipline to understand how money behaves and how systems grow.

The athlete who develops this muscle early does not have to become an exception.
He becomes an example.

The System Behind the System

Wealthy families win because they build systems.

They build:

- trusts
- corporations
- real estate portfolios
- cashflow machines
- tax strategies
- operational teams
- long-term plans that outlive individual careers

Athletes are taught to build moments.
Systems require them to build futures.

When he learns this, he stops thinking like talent and starts thinking like ownership.

Ownership is not about ego.
It is about stability.
It is about creating a foundation that does not collapse when the spotlight does.

Cashflow Is the Real Contract

Most athletes chase the wrong numbers.

They look at:

- salary
- bonuses
- endorsements
- followers
- exposure
- short-term money

But the quiet millionaires focus on:

- rentals
- businesses
- equity
- operating companies
- intellectual property

- distributions
- recurring income

A contract ends.
Cashflow does not.

A career lasts a few years.
Cashflow lasts a lifetime.

He does not need millions to build it.
He needs structure, timing, and discipline.

Most athletes are told to build a brand.
Few are told to build a balance sheet.

When he learns this difference, the curve bends in his favor.

Examples No One Talks About

The public celebrates the superstar.
The system celebrates the outlier.
But the blueprint belongs to the men no one knows.

The role player who bought three duplexes a year and retired with a real estate portfolio.
The overseas guard who built a trucking company while playing internationally.
The practice squad receiver who opened two gyms and a physical therapy clinic.
The backup point guard who invested in vending

routes and scaled them.
The defensive lineman who acquired franchises quietly and built generational income.
The journeyman who turned his per diem into a rental property empire.

No parades.
No headlines.
No documentaries.

Just systems.
Just structure.
Just ownership.

These men prove one truth.

Wealth does not require fame.
It requires strategy.

The Advisors Who Build or Break the Future

Athletes do not fail alone.
They fail with help.

They fail with:

- advisors who do not educate
- accountants who do not explain
- agents who maximize short-term contracts
- friends who mismanage money
- teams who discourage business focus
- networks who weaponize visibility

Building differently means building a team with aligned incentives.

He needs advisors who teach him, not replace him.
Accountants who explain the numbers.
Attorneys who protect ownership.
Mentors who have receipts, not opinions.

No one can build alone.
But he must choose people who are building for him, not through him.

The Quiet Discipline That Separates the Few

Building differently requires a mindset that rarely gets applause.

He has to be willing to:

- live below the lifestyle his fame suggests
- delay gratification
- invest before he impresses
- learn what ownership actually means
- build when no one is paying attention
- protect himself from the noise
- choose long-term structure over short-term validation

This is not glamorous.
But it is what creates stability long after the last game.

The athlete who understands this early does not fear the cliff.
He prepares for it.

The Line That Defines This Chapter

He was taught to perform.
He was taught to entertain.
He was taught to spend.

No one taught him to build.

The path to building differently begins the moment he learns the truth:

A lifestyle ends when the checks do.
A system continues long after he does.

CHAPTER 15: THE HUNDRED MILLION THAT NEVER EXISTED

The Autopsy of an Illusion

He signs the contract, and the world believes he is rich.
Rich forever.
Set for life.
Walking into a future his family never touched.

The number hits the headlines.
One hundred million dollars.

That is the moment the illusion begins.

No one explains that the number on the screen is not the number that builds a future.
No one explains that the contract is not cash.
No one explains that the system designed the contract to look bigger than it is.

He signs.
The world celebrates.
The truth hides.

This is the gap between perception and reality.
This is the hundred million that never existed.

The Composite Story That Mirrors Thousands

He is twenty-two.
He cannot legally rent a car in some states.
He is handed a contract worth more than everyone he grew up around will ever see combined.

He thinks it is his.
It is not.

He thinks he earned it.
He did, but he does not control it.

He thinks he is safe.
He is not.

Because the hundred million the public sees is not the hundred million he keeps.
It is not the hundred million he uses.
It is not the hundred million that builds generational wealth.

It is the number that sells the story of success.
A story that hides the architecture of extraction.

The Math They Never Show You

Break it down.

Line one: one hundred million.
Line two: guaranteed money.
Line three: taxes in every state he plays.
Line four: agent fee.

Line five: NFL, NBA, MLB union dues.
Line six: trainer, chef, off-season prep.
Line seven: financial advisor.
Line eight: family support.
Line nine: debt repayment for childhood sacrifices.
Line ten: lifestyle inflation created by fame.
Line eleven: short career window.
Line twelve: no compounding behind him.

By the time he retires, that hundred million becomes:

thirty-five million
then twenty-three million
then fourteen million
then nine million
then five million
then sometimes less than one.

And that is assuming he never made one mistake, never overspent, never trusted the wrong person, never got injured, never became the financial savior for anyone around him.

The world calls it mismanagement.
The system calls it normal.

The Cultural Forces Behind the Numbers

He comes from a curve that started late.
He comes from a family that depended on him before he ever saw a paycheck.

He comes from a history where success feels like a shared responsibility.
He comes from a community where opportunities were uneven but expectations were not.

He steps into a world where:

- he must provide
- he must rescue
- he must represent
- he must elevate
- he must protect
- he must absorb the weight of everyone who helped him survive childhood

The hundred million is not a hundred million.
It is the combined pressure of generations.

People think the danger is spending.
The danger is believing he ever truly had the money people said he did.

The System That Knows Exactly What It Is Doing

Every dollar he earns passes through a structure that was built long before he arrived.

He takes the physical risk.
The league takes the revenue.
The networks take the upside.
The owners take the equity.

The sponsors take the visibility.
The institutions take the legacy.

He gets paid to perform.
Everyone else gets paid because he performs.

The media plays a role in the illusion.

They announce the contract value as if it were cash.

They headline the biggest number because it sells the story.

They never follow up on the real breakdown.

They never explain the guaranteed portion.

They never explain the taxes or the short career window.

They never explain the cultural obligations.

The number becomes a myth repeated so loudly that even the athlete begins to believe it.

People judge him by a figure that never reflected his reality.

The curve behind him did not compound.
The system in front of him compounds against him.

This is what people miss when they ask,

"How do you lose a hundred million dollars?"

He never had a hundred million to lose.

The Financial Cliff Hidden in Plain Sight

Contract lengths shrink.
Guaranteed money shrinks.
Career windows shrink.
Bodies decline.
Opportunities fade.
Visibility drops.
Endorsements vanish.
Expenses remain.
Dependents remain.
Expectations remain.

The number goes away.
The obligations do not.

He arrives at thirty-three years old with the same pressure he felt at twenty-two and one-twentieth of the income.

It is not a collapse.
It is a countdown.

A countdown that began the day he signed the contract.

The Moment He Realizes the Truth

There is always a moment.

A declined endorsement deal.
A contract negotiation that goes silent.
A new rookie drafted at his position.
A younger, cheaper version of him rising quickly.
A call from an advisor he cannot trust anymore.
A bill he did not expect.
A family emergency, he is expected to solve.

The moment he realizes the hundred million was never there is the moment he understands the game behind the game.

He was taught to play.
He was never taught to own.

The Line That Defines This Chapter

The world celebrates the number on the contract.
The truth is found in the math that comes after it.
What people call a collapse was only the illusion running out.

CHAPTER 16: THE NEW BLUEPRINT FOR FIRST-GENERATION ATHLETES

The Blueprint That Was Never Given

History rarely explains itself.
It simply repeats in new uniforms.

Long before a young athlete signed his first NIL deal or posed on draft night, this story was already being written.
Black talent has always been visible.
Black ownership has never been protected.

On plantations, Black bodies were valued for output, not opportunity.
In early boxing, fighters filled arenas they could not even sit in outside the ring.
In segregated leagues, Black athletes broke records but were denied contracts, equity, pensions, and pathways.
Even in the modern era, billions in revenue have flowed through stadiums, broadcasts, shoe deals, media rights, and global merchandising built on Black excellence, yet the ownership tables remain almost entirely unchanged.

The system evolved.
The uniforms evolved.
The money evolved.
The structure did not.

This is why first-generation athletes walk into a world built on their talent but not designed for their long-term stability.

They inherit visibility, not leverage.
Fame, not ownership.
Income, not literacy.
Opportunity, not protection.
And a financial curve that begins and ends entirely on their back.

The blueprint they needed was never given to them.
So this chapter builds it.

The Myths that Protect the System

Myth 1: "Athletes make enough money."
This myth depends on the public never learning the math.
Income is not wealth.
A short career is not security.
Visibility is not ownership.

Myth 2: "NIL fixes everything."
NIL gives teenagers money inside a system that still gives them no education, no protection, and no

long-term plan.
It is access without guardrails.

Myth 3: "If the stars succeeded, anyone can."
Media showcases unicorns to distract from the system that fails the majority.
A few meteors do not define the sky.

Myth 4: "Financial failure equals personal failure."
This myth hides the truth: the structure is designed for fast turnover, short windows, high pressure, and low literacy.

Myth 5: "The system already supports them."
Everyone is paid from their talent.
Very few are paid to protect their future.

The myths collapse when the truth arrives.
So now we build the new blueprint.

The New Blueprint for First-Generation Athletes

This blueprint is not a dream.
It is a system that can be taught, modeled, and repeated.

The heart of it is ownership.
The structure around it is cultural.
The execution of it is personal.
The responsibility for it is collective.

Below are the principles, short, sharp, and foundational, followed by practical explanation.

The Ownership Principles

Principle 1: Income is temporary. Ownership is permanent.
A contract ends.
Equity compounds.
The system thrives when athletes chase income instead of ownership.

Principle 2: Take one percent of something powerful over one hundred percent of something fragile.
A minority stake in infrastructure outlives a decade of endorsement deals.

Principle 3: Build slow money before you touch fast money.
If the foundation is weak, the windfall becomes destruction.

Principle 4: Wealth grows in the dark, not the spotlight.
The public sees the celebration, not the compounding.

Principle 5: The first decision is the most expensive one.
The team you hire will shape your life more than the team you play for.

Principle 6: Ownership begins with literacy.
A person cannot protect what they cannot define.

Principle 7: Make decisions the future version of you will thank you for.
Not the version standing in the spotlight.
The version standing in silence.

Policy-Level Guidelines

These are systemic changes that would protect athletes if institutions adopted them.

1. NIL trusts for minors
A percentage locked until age twenty-one, tied to literacy requirements.

2. Mandatory financial education written by unbiased experts
Not advisors who profit from the athletes they teach.

3. Cap on advisor fees and transparent auditing
Standardized oversight to remove hidden predatory structures.

4. Ownership pathways inside leagues
Educational pipelines to team equity, not just contract renewals.

5. Mandatory transition programs starting at year one
Not after a career ends, when it is too late.

These are not radical.
They are reasonable.

Cultural Guidelines for Parents, Coaches, and Mentors

1. Stop celebrating early access. Celebrate early discipline.
Early fame requires early structure.

2. Teach responsibility before visibility.
Carry your own bag before carrying a program.

3. Stop selling the child to every opportunity.
Protect the pipeline, or it becomes a trap.

4. Build identity outside the sport.
Your purpose cannot end when the cheering ends.

5. Teach the difference between attention and value.
One is public.
One is private.
The latter builds wealth.

The Personal Blueprint for Every Athlete

This is where the steps become real.

Step 1: Build a literacy team before a lifestyle team.
One good CPA is worth more than ten brand endorsements.

Step 2: Automate protection.
Trusts, insurance, budgets, oversight, build systems that protect you from emotion and pressure.

Step 3: Put twenty percent into ownership vehicles immediately.
It can be small.
It must be consistent.

Step 4: Treat your first contract like it is your last.
Because statistically, it probably is.

Step 5: Do not build for applause. Build for exit.
What remains after the spotlight fades is what matters.

Step 6: Learn negotiation.
Not the public part.
The ownership part.
The equity part.

Step 7: Build a business that makes money when you do not.
Your body is not a retirement plan.

The Cultural Shift

This is bigger than one athlete.

Black wealth is not built by lone stars.
It is built by communities that understand ownership.

Parents must shift.
Coaches must shift.
Schools must shift.
Agents must shift.
Athletes must shift.

No one is behind.
We were simply never shown the path.

Until now.

The Destiny Ending

The system will not change itself.
The blueprint must spread through culture, family, mentorship, and community.

This chapter is not a warning.
It is a foundation.

A new generation of athletes is rising.
Athletes who will enter the spotlight with literacy.
With structure.
With ownership.
With protection.

With clarity.
With a blueprint they did not have to invent on their own.

The next era of Black wealth will not depend on miracles.
It will depend on systems.
It will depend on truth.
It will depend on the courage to build differently.

And now the blueprint exists.

The Iconic Closing Line

The curve breaks the moment he learns that the real game was never played on the court. It was played in the decisions he makes once the world stops cheering.

AFTER THE APPLAUSE

He sits alone in the same gym where he once swept the floor on a Tuesday night, the night the world had forgotten him.
The lights hum softly above.
The scoreboard is dark again.
But the silence feels different now.

The first time he stood here, silence felt like punishment.
Tonight, it feels like clarity.

He is older by a few years.
Not old in a way the world would recognize.
Old in a way only an athlete understands.
Old in the places that once carried the weight of a dream too heavy for one person.

He drops a worn leather bag next to the bench.
Not the kind a brand paid him to carry.
Just a simple work bag filled with papers, a notebook, and a laptop that hums with spreadsheets, he is finally learning how to read.

No cameras.
No stylists.
No team handlers moving around him.

For the first time, he is the one managing his own life.

He glances at the far end of the court.
A teenage kid is shooting alone.
Awkward form.
Big dreams.
Wearing a pair of shoes that cost more than the family who bought them could afford.

He recognizes the story instantly.

He walks over, rebounds a missed shot, and passes the ball back.

The kid looks shocked.
Not because of who he is.
But because adults rarely stop to help without asking for anything in return.

They talk.
Not long.
Not loud.
Just enough for the kid to understand one truth no one ever told him.

"It is not about how far talent takes you," he says quietly.
"It is about what you build while you still have it."

He does not talk about millions.
He does not talk about fame.
He does not talk about endorsement deals or the years he spent drowning in expectations.

He talks about discipline.
He talks about choices.

He talks about the mistakes that nearly cost him everything.
He talks about carrying burdens he did not understand until it was too late to drop them.

And then he talks about something almost no one ever told him.

"Build something that lasts longer than the applause."

The kid nods.
He does not fully understand yet.
But the seed is planted.

Later, long after the kid leaves, he sits at center court with the papers from his bag spread around him.
They are not contracts.
They are not endorsement proposals.
They are not media requests.

They are plans.

Ownership plans.
Small, steady, unglamorous steps toward a life that will not disappear when the world moves on.

He signs documents for the first percentage of a local business he believes in.
Not a flashy investment.
Not a quick flip.
But something with weight.

Something that can grow quietly.
Something he can pass down.

He closes the folder and leans back on his hands, staring at the ceiling lights.

This time, the quiet does not scare him.
It prepares him.

He thinks about the years he chased applause, not understanding that applause has no memory.
He thinks about how fast one hundred million can move through a life when the life was never taught how to hold it.
He thinks about the boy he used to be, the one the system praised for what he could do but never prepared for what came after.

Then he smiles.

Because he finally understands something he wishes he had known all along.

The world celebrates the rise.
The world dramatizes the fall.
But the real life, the meaningful life, begins here in the calm nobody watches.

This is not the comeback.
This is not redemption.
This is not the miracle story people love to share.

This is the beginning.

This is ownership taking its first quiet breath.

Here, in an empty gym, after the applause has gone home, he is building the part of the curve no one taught him.
The part he will one day teach to someone else.

The part that was missing the whole time.

AUTHOR'S NOTE

This book was not written to criticize athletes.
It was written to protect them.

For years, I have watched stories about Black athletes fold into the same predictable narrative.
A young star rises.
A young star shines.
A young star loses everything.
People point, judge, shake their head, and move on.

But no one ever stops to ask the real question.
Why does this keep happening?

The easy answers were never good enough for me.
I never believed the collapse was simply bad budgeting or reckless spending or a lack of discipline.
I have lived long enough and seen enough to know that anyone who believes those explanations has never carried the weight of being first.
First to make it.
First to leave home.
First to have money.
First to be depended on by everyone around you.

This book is for the athletes who never stood a chance at stability because no one taught them the truth behind the machine.
It is for the families who sacrificed everything without ever receiving a roadmap.

It is for the parents who loved the dream but did not know the cost.
It is for the coaches who meant well but could only teach what they had been taught.
It is for the young men who were praised for their bodies but never prepared for the business their bodies were walking into.

I wrote this because I have seen what happens when someone reaches the top of a system built without them in mind.
I have seen what it feels like to be celebrated publicly and confused privately.
I have seen the pressure of being the first one to hold money in a family that has never had the chance to understand it.
I have seen the silence that follows the applause.

What these athletes face is not personal failure.
It is historical.
It is structural.
It is generational.
And it is invisible until the moment it collapses.

This book is not about judgment.
It is about context.
It is about culture.
It is about the truth that connects the past to the present.
It is about understanding that one hundred million dollars can disappear when the education, the protection, the infrastructure, and the ownership were never built in the first place.

I wrote this so the next generation does not walk into the same darkness.
I wrote this because someone has to explain the part of the story that the media does not tell.
I wrote this because these young men are not cautionary tales.
They are the products of a curve that started long before they were born.

And I wrote this because I believe in them.
Deeply.
Quietly.
Without reservation.

If this book does anything, I hope it shifts the narrative from blame to understanding, from judgment to preparation, and from collapse to ownership.
We are not behind.
We were simply never shown the game behind the game.

This is the beginning of that correction.

This book belongs to the larger mission that began with The Black Wealth Papers and Why You Are Not Behind. Those pages started a conversation about reframing the curve and reclaiming our place inside it. This volume continues that work by focusing on the corner of the culture most praised and most misunderstood. The goal has not changed. The responsibility has not changed. The truth has not changed. We are still correcting the story, one chapter at a time.

ACKNOWLEDGMENTS

Books like this are never written alone.
They are carried by every conversation, every observation, and every person who helped reveal the truth behind the stories we were taught to accept without question.

To the athletes who opened their lives to the world, who carried dreams bigger than their resources, who endured praise and criticism with the same quiet strength, this book is for you. Your journeys shaped every chapter. Your courage shaped every truth that lives in these pages.

To the families who supported young athletes long before cameras arrived, who poured time, money, and belief into a dream they could not fully understand, thank you. You built the foundation before anyone knew it was a foundation.

To the parents, coaches, and mentors who care enough to teach what they were never taught, your work matters more than you will ever receive credit for. The next generation will rise because of you.

To the men and women who have challenged systems, corrected narratives, and fought to create ownership pathways where none existed, this book stands on the work you began.

To everyone who has ever felt behind, overwhelmed, or unprepared, the message remains the same. You were never behind. You were simply never given the blueprint. The responsibility and the opportunity are ours now.

And finally, to the readers who continue to support The Black Wealth Papers and the mission that began with Why You Are Not Behind, thank you for choosing to learn, to question, and to grow. These books exist because you understand the importance of building truthfully. We are rewriting the curve together.

Made in the USA
Monee, IL
04 November 2026

67384047R00079